Real Stories

GARETH REEVES

Real Stories

CARCANET

For Carole, Jessica and Samuel

Some of the poems in this collection first appeared in the following publications, to whose editors acknowledgement is due: *Encounter, Intro 4* (University Press of Virginia), *The Literary Review, London Magazine, Makaris, New Poetry 1975* (*Critical Quarterly* poetry supplement No. 16), *New Statesman, Outposts, P.N. Review, Scotsman, Ten English Poets* (Carcanet, 1976). "Church-wall" was broadcast on BBC *Radio 3*.

Every effort has been made to trace copyright for the cover photograph by Charles Eames of Simon Rodia's Watts Towers, Los Angeles.

First published in 1984 by
Carcanet Press Limited
208-212 Corn Exchange Buildings
Manchester M4 3BQ

British Library Cataloguing in Publication Data
Reeves, Gareth
Real Stories.
I. Title
821'.914   PR6068.E39
ISBN 0-85635-520-8

The publisher acknowledges the financial assistance
of the Arts Council of Great Britain.

Typeset by Bryan Williamson, Todmorden
Printed by SRP Ltd, Exeter

Contents

I

II

III

I

Horace I,11: Tu ne quaesieris

Don't ask, you must not know, Leuconoë,
About the end gods give to me, to you.
Don't fool with horoscopes. Take what comes.
We may have many winters, or our last
Now tires the Tyrrhene sea against the rocks;
And so take thought, take wine. As life is short
Prune back long hopes. Time, jealous of our talk,
Goes. Gather the day. It may be your last.

The Garden

How close the wood-dove sounds against your ear
Each morning early with its dreary burr,
Repeating your dilemma on the air.
You have built up ambitious solitude;
Your walled-in garden swells with plant and life.
Fat pigeons, enigmatic tortoises,
Knurled branches twisting in the summer sun,
Espaliered pears suspending their full fruit—
All blur and blear in your myopic eye.
  Your world is constantly alive, now that
Your wife is dead; each movement in the grass,
Each bird-call, each susurrus, is your theme.
You hear your heart-beat in your terraced world,
Where crumbling Cotswold wall holds back the earth
And threatens to collapse, but never does.
Your reach of love is now your stretch of lawn.
  Closer and closer I come; the picture blurs.
I watch your rich enigmas gather round,
Shade upon shade: gnarled hand, lined eye,
The wrinkled cheek, the silent, down-turned mouth,
Creases and crevices that do not speak
Except of age, but hint at the hidden, father.

ii.

Cadences fill the garden. They are yours:
Birdnotes at dusk descending from your trees,
Water trickling down unpointed brick.
All night I hear the garden running down.
  You gardened once. Roses for her you pruned:
Parkman, and other names I have forgotten.
Only what grows untended now you plant:
Rockeries, trees, and lawns where flowers grew—
Easy to care for, and to let run wild.

iii.

Convolvulus grips your garden.
What I am and what I might have been
Are nothing here.
Your will twists round my words.
Anger is useless. Recrimination
Gets no further than my throat.

iv.

Don't say it now, I cannot, it is too late.
Rancour declines to richness.
Teach me your patience, garden.
Regret is irrelevant; teach me
Not to regret the words we never spoke.
Teach the son
That honesty is difficult,
Devious, silent.

Stills

i.m. M.R.

I

The photo of you I have
by heart: you in a deckchair
casting a clear shadow
on garden flag-stones where
crab-grass has not yet pushed through.

Poised, smile faintly bewildered,
you are enduring something,
watching past my shoulder
a landscape I know well:
sea-glint, green estuary,

oxbow, a distant hill;
behind you a French window
with silvered panes, ajar
to a dark inside, where stilled
shapes are about to stir.

II

Often when I think of you
it is that photo, taken late.
After your death
he can't have thought of you
like that. He resurrected
a portrait done in your late twenties
when your mind was on soldiers
and Ceylon; you took him on the rebound,
he said. He heard of you
through friends, a beauty,
unobtainable—until he got you;
after that he was your slightly stern
stand-offish schoolmaster,
a change from the others, he said.

Your version doesn't exist,
except in silence:
your hands stopped
over some household task,
an absent look.

III

From this distance you are,
I suppose, not as you were
but as I would have you.

I recall sun on a window-sill,
you silhouetted, reading novel
after novel. Did you live

in books, in those quiet
mid-morning lulls you had
to yourself?—that life I touch
only as photographs.

IV

Italy—a chance to indulge
your liking for canals and cannelloni,
Canalettos, Guardis, madonnas,
Caravaggios and piètas!

Your son-in-law may have
chased her round the Trevi Fountain—
the bottom-pinching sort
whose short mamma stokes him
with spaghetti done al dente
as an antipasto, and remembers
all the others her carissimo
brought home without getting hooked—

but here it was, your first
grandchild, a squalling six-month-old
bambina. You must have sighed
as you cradled it
in your English arms.
In a few days you died.

V

Your body from Italy, mine from Greece
to a homecoming I did not want;
yours in the hold, mine

hanging in air, all movement
gone, all thought but one,
an absence that clings,
a solid cloud, through which

the plane plunges and rocks
till the ground comes up
and we bounce and skid to a dead
stop amid rushing silence.

Intruders

Up from Italy by Beetle
piled high with pasta,
salami, coffee-beans ("the English,
they don't know how to eat well"),
most of it gone stale on the way,
they parked one night
below the high flint wall, and tapped
at the picture-window unannounced.

Father sat half-listening
to Vivaldi. He blinked and stared.
What to do with these midnight visitors
with their tramontane ways,
grousing in bad English about
warm beer and the weather?

A week, and they drove back
after hearty handshakes
and the obligatory embrace.
The son remained.
He was my father's son now.
He'd made his bed. He'd lie in it...

A few years later he upped and left
B-movie style, for mamma
or so we thought. Next Christmas
he returned without warning, was welcomed
as if from a weekend jaunt.
He never came again.

At a Funeral

Assume the undertaker's pose for death.
He must conduct:
every day for this he wears his tails,
polishes his baton, gesticulates
to his little orchestra.
And I have come before
with my tie butterflied against my neck
and a suave indifference;
attended the deaths of others in acoustics so correct
that harmony played havoc with my senses.

Homing In

One of your wry projects,
"The Unencyclopaedia
of Useless Information"—sole entry
"Napoleon had white eyebrows"—
gets fatter and funnier now.

Your hand—a wing hovering,
alighting, enfolding your whisky
glass to lift it short-sightedly
and check the depth while our talk
wavered and fumbled—would nudge
the bottle my way, smearing
the table with sticky spills,
and wave your cigar smoke
vaguely aside to return
the stub to the ashtray and pound
out one more paragraph...

your burn-marks on my desk—
here you reclined each day
comfortably paunched, singeing
wiry eyebrows with that
myopically adjusted
flame-throwing gas Ronson.

Theme and Variations

"The Harmonious Blacksmith", the only piece
I ever heard my father play—
he must have been practising it
when his sight failed. His hands spun
elaborate and endless variations,
filling the minutes, the half-hours
it took my mother to "get ready".

The tune comes to me for no reason,
as do the endless streets, the increasingly rare
car-less by-ways we trailed in foreign cities,
looking for the right café, quiet, no wind,
waiters polite, where he would practise
the difficult art of whiling away time,
waiting for small inspirations from passers-by
or from the couple two tables away
on whose conversation he would speculate
in a loud *sotto voce*,
making me squirm or sit rapt
by his inventions of episodes
in other people's lives, until his talk
was stunned into silence by the traffic,
or the light went
and it was time to guide him
down blind alleys back to the hotel.

The Mentor

Tending abstractions in your
prismatic head, your hand stroked
back imaginary hair.
Always anxious to shatter
some fine ray of truth, you kept
us listening through dinner.

Ash lengthened; fingers yellowed.
Arguments were hot, and you
switched sides quicker than it took
to take one swallow of your
well-cellared liquor. After-
dinner sleep came fast to all
but you, who mulled the subject
over with quiet laughter.

In this book now I have you
arguing with yourself, or
anyone. I read into
the night, and sentences blur.
Smoke fills my head; I recall
your jovial evenings.
On the page your phrases bulge
and swallowing them is hard.

England, my England

It was shot off giving the thumbs-up
as he led the charge over the hill-top;
he also said, since it's gone
it won't get hurt at the wicket
and makes a good excuse for lost catches.

Brandishing the shiny stub, prodding
the air, sometimes our ribs, with it,
he could still grab with fingers
and flexing palm the nearest ear,
nose or shying shoulder; and once

he got my hair: the tuft
glinted in his fist, then floated
through dust-motes to the floor.
Mother took me to the doctor
with suspected early balding; even now
my silence makes me scratch my head.

He did General Knowledge, the bullet
head jerking to quizzes on rugger,
stalagmites and -tites, the last
country to leave the Commonwealth,
on how many rivers called Ouse,
on populations of unlikely places

where he'd never set foot and didn't want to.
Stubbly moustache, eyes that poked
into a diminishing future, visions
of touch-lines and boundary fences,
he made a virtue of sanity

and was slightly off his head.
There he is, running up to bowl
in a deep green limbo, fingers
feeling the seam for off-spin or googly,
in a blue funk at the endless
journey across his elysium.

English Lesson

He is our fond teacher.
"This is where it happened, this
is the place." Stopping where
Perdita gives flowers to Florizel

he stands, legs slightly apart,
and remembers how they took him
one noon from the P.O.W. reading club
mid-speech ... Before the war he was engaged;

after it, he soaked in the bath for hours
slicing dead skin from his soles,
it is rumoured: shoes wore out
fast on the Burma railway.

When a shovel disappeared
someone stepped forward to own up
and was shot then and there;
then the shovel turned up ...

Stories for schoolboys—
his high-voiced and bitter
charity made real, I see now,
in the listening, childish faces.

Out of Bounds

Always the several entrances:
from the hall where we had pep-talks
on team-spirit and prayers after chips,
through a door at the back, past yards
of parquet, into that quiet;
or the garden passage, or the never used
dark stairs from the attic "squealers"
down to the ground floor—the high
voices of his daughters floating up.

The feel of other lives next to our own:
a First in Modern Languages, then travel
and marriage to a very neat Frenchwoman:
only once do I recall him letting fly,
about "that blackamoor who blew a bubble
in the front row of the House photograph."
He dreaded the day his daughters would arise
as beauties on a sea of scrambling schoolboys.

He did not survive the car-crash one summer
somewhere in the Massif Central.
His family did; they were sucked back
into France with their memories: bemused
on the sideline in a surge of pent-up boys,
mother and daughters watching as bare limbs
jinxed and tackled across an English pitch.

Can We Interest You in God?

"Do you have a Bible in the house?"
"My husband has written a new version
thank you" she says, and firmly shuts the door.
Craning over the banister, I'm proud.
Could your mum come up with a line like that?

"See me afterwards, I'll tell you my method"
the chaplain says. So I go. "Leaving us soon
for the big world, are you? Remember God.
Where to now?" "A month or so in Paris
before I go up." (I'm pleased with that last phrase.)
"Er... take this *A Prayer a Day*... try not to..."

What's he thinking of? The *Moulin Rouge*?
Plastic macs in the Latin Quarter?
That's nothing on the boy at school
found naked under another boy's bed: "O Sir,
you see Sir, I lost my way to the loo."
He was expelled for that caper.

My dad's *The Holy Bible in Brief*—
I don't think he believed a word of it:
he cut out the difficult bits
and stuck to the story. Never mind the meaning.

End of Term Report

"Let me see... the name is..." turning
the pages. "H'm, not getting any worse, not getting
any better." Still turning, "Ahem."

Ahem. He dilates on how
he can tell the character of a chap
from his performance on the rugger-pitch.

Play the clarinet? "I have a son
who conducts. Fine thing, music."
He shoots out a hand.

This is goodbye. I flinch:
his little finger's missing. Grasp it.
Otherwise you've failed the test.

The Graduate Trainees Take Off

"Get yourself a drink." I fumble
the bottles, take a sip, and wince: it's gin

and soda… I try not to be noticed.
He tries not to notice: "And how are things

in Mailing?" (Nothing to write home about.
Last week someone grabbed his brolly

and left—to go to the Gents,
so he said. He was never seen again.)

At the round table each thinks of the quest,
something to say. No food comes:

he grips the edge (a breakdown? a fit?),
but relaxes when the salvers arrive.

A silver cover lifts off—to reveal
supine potatoes. After the meal

we are stranded on the carpet,
high flyers, herons on one leg.

Where he clutched the table
I spy a hidden push-button.

Regret

People my verses do not teem with hurt
more than the fleshed-out memories
that get to them.

Past words, flesh-touches clutch,
recede, leaving the mind
blanker than mind can contemplate.

I would be Aeneas
but the shades that haunt me
do not turn to marble. They wander

formless and forming in the mind still.
I have tried Lethe and the upper air;
each time regret pushes me back again.

Bridge on the River Kwai

Whistling in step on the loud boards
they march until they are larger than life
to the edge of the screen and then off

into silence, the dead pause
when lights come up and you feel
you have arrived at a conviction

which slips away in the hubbub
outside dimly approaching
as you exit to bar or bus-stop.

You try to pin it down.
The plan seems easy enough:
that whatever he did would have been

wrong and right, that losing his grip
would have cost in the end more courage
than keeping it, that a helicopter thudding

down through the jungle and a silent posse
to blow up the bridge had got the Director
out of a jam and the story ended.

You know too that a *deus ex machina*
won't descend, that real stories
do not conclude but merely stop

anywhere, when the celluloid snaps
and the projector's flip-flip
goes round and round and on and on

drifting like the street-sounds
you walk hypnotically towards
in an army of ghosts.

Blackberry Pickers

You stretch with your heads far in
sniffing a dry-cellar sweetness,
flesh caught in the brambles

to touch that unreachable
berry which drops in the palm
and leaves a conical stalk-head

nodding, or which bursts black
compact lobes down your fingers
in sticky unlickable

stains that sting your scratches.
Often the best to taste now,
by the bushes, are the ones dulled

by a dust-and-dirt bloom;
but the particoloured dark and red
are just as tempting: today

they may be a bit tart
but tomorrow somebody else
will pick them, jet all over.

Edging and inching
you hope to strip the bush
to the last berry, leaving

none for the birds or the future;
but you know you never will
for there's always another

lurking, like all the other
unfound berries which now you find
at the last moment, when you say

"The basket's full, let's go."
And as you leave with pips
in your teeth, trying not to take

one more final look, you imagine
unpicked berries turning black
and you not there to pick them.

II

Horace I,37: Nunc est bibendum

Now, friends, drink,
now beat the earth with free foot,
now with Salarian feast furnish the gods' couches.

Once it was wrong to raid
ancestors' cellars for Caecuban,
once, when the queen, with her rabble of eunuchs,
those virile adventurers,
drunk with sweet fortune and madly daring the world
made crazy ruin of the Capitol
and a grave of empire.

Return of scarce a ship from the fire's roar
diminished her mania. Caesar sobered her
whom Mareotic wine had made mad.

He fettered that monster of fate; she
sought death with nobility.
She did not shudder at swords like a woman,
nor did her ships retreat to hidden shores.

Calmly she risked a last look at her flattened palace,
steadfastly clutched sharp-toothed snakes
that her veins might drink deep the dark venom;

no lowly woman, she,
ferocious now death had been fixed on,
scorned to be led by barbaric Liburnians
unqueened in arrogant triumph.

Central Valley, California
for Steve and Marsha Shankman

The centre-line flicks at me
and rebounds in the rear-view mirror.
I drive my appurtenances,
slant-six and battered body,
my headlights out of whack—
but it's not night now—
my raucous Plymouth, bent
and patched-up piece of America,
into this desert valley.
The antenna shakes as the wheels
judder over the cracked tarmac.
The broken-down radio,
its loose connections jumping,
bursts into life, goes dead, bursts again
into a Savings and Loan ad, "guaranteed
federally up to forty-thousand",
then a baroque sonata.

I drive past mountains
bristling on the skyline with dead trees,
hillocks in the foreground
stippled with browns and greys,
past tentacular roots sticking out of the sand
and rocks wind-tortured into fat
birds, faces of old men, noses, a hand:
a bomb-site in the sun's equal glare,
a landscape ravaged by the eye.

There should be ghosts here
and I try to see them:
of pioneers, of gold-prospectors;
and those who stalked invisible paths,
ghosts of a ghosted race, with whom I share

too little of their trampled rituals.
But it's no good,
even the word "ghost" seems out of place.
No one is here; unreal
America spreads its wave-bands
over a desert air.
My alien eye
conjures a violence from nowhere.

Rat Race

"Stroke it. Stroke. Don't
for God's sake let it go."
Too late. It clawed, drew blood,
rapped and skidded on vinyl,
then skulked behind cupboards.
"That one'll be nervy
for at least six weeks now."

Our neighbour had a wife and a white
rat that slept in the bottom drawer,
usurping underwear and socks.
Rats in a maze: he couldn't bear
to make the sleek albino
chase cheese down corridors of wire.
The landlord ("pets forbidden")
never saw the rat. It was too quick.
Eventually our neighbour was evicted
for painting a giant eye
on the bedroom window—to stop, he said,
the couple in the apartment opposite
peering in.
                    His research topic
was overcrowding. When the cages
bulged rats, would they fight,
turn cannibal, make love, go mad?
(He said he could tell a mad rat.)
From this, of course, the human situation.
But we are no more rats
than naked apes, I thought.
Then he escaped to a Tanzanian
rainforest to study the chimpanzee.

I think of him in his old
oil-squirting car, cruising the Bay Area's
tangle of freeways: the sun-glinting steel,

the bumper-to-bumper drone,
eyes behind glass deliberately
not looking into other eyes,
friendly, unseeing, alone.

Californian Sounds

A drop-out Sociology Ph.D.,
the walls of his clapboard shack
lined with all the books
he had not sold yet ("they make
good insulation") and a squat-dog
pioneer stove with the flue
straight up like a cocked tail
to keep him company—

he meant to retreat, to think and write
about the individual in society,
and came to ground in a sea
of field-grass and hay-stubble,
seed misting the horizon to a brown haze.
He listened to his thoughts and the bamboo
shifting, the sharp leaves
scraping together, hedging him in...

Finally he made it into print
in *The Last Whole Earth Catalog*
selling hand-whittled Shakuhachi flutes
world wide. He sawed and reamed and trimmed,
then sat cross-legged for days
perfecting his embouchure
until the thin notes were suddenly there,
easing and bending from the stout bamboo.
The last we heard he had jetted
across the Pacific, a Shakuhachi
contract in his breast-pocket.

Pugilistic

He knocks his man down nimbly,
knowing by knack the exact spot
to put his foot for the gliding fulcrum,
brain in his fists and brawn compacted
to the logic of a direct hit.
And now he meets the lens, the hullabaloo—
no rebounding from slung ropes
or bouncing on the balls of his feet,
so he parries with an "I am the Greatest".
But words won't work for him
a shield of fisticuffs. He looks
baffled for an instant, eyes and face
open to all hurt; then the chin
comes up, and the bludgeoning grin.

California Drift

A bobbing aluminium
Beer-can nudges the river-bank.
Across the shallows the deep wood
Absorbs a moody thrum:
Someone plucks at random—
No serenade to bodices
Bowing from a rabbit-warren
Forty-niner's brothel, now
A hotel of exhausted beds.

The girls are asleep for good.
Eddies glint and blur:
The moon is panning gold.
Voices of guests behind clapboard
Fade out and in, soothe and threaten
Like a low-power radio,
Making sense but not in words.
It could be any language anywhere.

To the left an empire died
In the heads of a few Russian
Sea-dogs who nosed the coast
For years, inlet by inlet:
Vladivostok, the Aleutians,
Fort Ross, Vancouver, Anchorage,
Eureka, Mendocino, Manchester...
The wide Pacific edge.

When in the prematurely dark
Bar on the main drag a man
'Mooned' at us, we walked out scared
Into a silver light that shone
On board-walk, shack shop, grey fir-trees,
The square head of a nineteen-fifties
Gas-pump, pot-holed macadam;
A deer was levitating in
The headlights of a slowing car.

The can gurgles and settles. Soon
The sun will come up on the right
Having crossed a continent
In one day, the yellow miles...
Okies and drop-outs drift
And fetch up here. All night
They tap their frets and hum
To themselves their marginal tunes.

Melting-pot

Green scars glimmer in El Camino Real's
architectural overkill: Spanish stucco
massage-parlours rub shoulders with ticky-tac
Tudor steak-houses and Disneyland motels:
the Cinderella Inn is a giant shoe.
The President once helicoptered over:
"And when light industry replaces orchards..."—
the royal way! "Survivors will be Prosecuted"
jokes a No Trespassing sign. We hope it jokes.
LUV U.C.B.—or else—is a car's number-plate.
A feminist collective sells home-made ice-cream
with frozen smiles. Above the hot macadam
banks, bars, realtors, poolrooms, waver in the pyre.
Next to a Szechwan restaurant a green billboard:
"Invest in Ireland, Europe's Silicon Valley".
H. Salt & Co., sporting the London Underground
with a map that has no blue Victoria Line,
sells wedges of Iceland cod in cardboard trays
printed with the Gothic, front-page-personal *Times*.

Avenues of Palm, of Indian Catalpa,
Australian Eucalyptus... Outside our house
a primitive Ginkgo waves its Japanese fans.
The Dutchman next door fishes below the snowline
in lakes called Honey, Josephine, Suzie, Big Jack.
Wobbling at the top of a telegraph pole
he shouts down, "Here in America you are free
to make your own electrical connections."
Jewish, they came over when the war started;
her father was an undertaker. Much remains
unspoken between us. Our German landlady
turned up after the war, the husband before it;
it is said that he preferred his bachelor days
on the porch-steps with his bottle and squeeze-box.

There's a grown son by her first marriage, silent,
eyes unfocussed, head shaven and to one side.
The attic has a tin trunk lined with *Der Führer*,
'38, picturing kindergarten children
perfectly behaved; in the letter pages
English blimps from Malta and Beaconsfield
make overtures in German translatorese;
and on the cover, there he is, saluting,
looking exactly like his caricature.

To a Much-travelled Friend

You, in your metropolitan attire,
Tamer of cities, lover
Of pavements at night in bizarre
Cafés, the curious rover,

Diner-out at hidden restaurants
With select acquaintance
In Europe's capitals, piquant
Raconteur, each nuance

Of your night-long eloquence
Giving the moment
A tone of consequence,

A dilettante, unsystematic,
You bathe in limpid air,
Gliding through Europe with aquatic
Ease, to seek your somewhere.

You attend the opera to hear
Artful bravura,
Especially the Rhine-maidens'
Defiant sprezzatura,

And feel at times a Götterdämmerung
While watching famous rivers,
When an evening gold is flung
Upon romantic waters.

You are the taster of some vague desire,
Gourmet of many faiths,
Able, with prospect of a spire
Glimpsed through architraves,

To let transparent days inspire
You to rhapsodic
Contemplation of a holy fire
Imagined and aesthetic.

Talker, watcher, taster, unbeliever,
You are the constant friend,
Who, among the ruins you revere,
Will always honour feelings to the end.

Pepper-tree

Green globes I crush and smell...
On the other side of the world
Domestic pepper-corn
Stung my nostrils until
Vague islands swam in my veins.

No wind, no ripple shifts
These delicate, barbed leaves
Like fishbone-skeletons:
Fish out of water, spines
Bared to a steely sun.

III

Catullus 2: Passer deliciae meae puellae

Sparrow, my mistress's truelove,
playmate she likes to hold in her lap,
and give her finger-tip
to provoke your sharp nips,
when my seductive darling
likes to play strange games with you,
and even, I think, satisfies her yearning,
quenching her passion: ah sparrow,
I wish my playing with you as she does
would soothe my achings also.

A Slawkenbergian Tale

"We're writing an article on sons
of well-known dads. Can we do you?"
"But that's like interviewing someone
with a bent nose: it's something you can't help."
(No *esprit d'escalier* now, for once.)
"Er... well... can we print that?" "No."

I'm violently doing the twist
with a girl I've never met before.
Drink splashes the floor. "You went head
over heels and landed on your nose"
she is saying as I come round, blood
blossoming on her frilly white blouse.

"A hairline fracture. An operation
wouldn't work. Breathe okay? Good. That'll be all"
and out I go. "At least there's the girl"
I think. But she only liked men
with bloody noses. Today mine's slightly bent.

The Nothing that Is

Sometimes a great land-mass splits off
and drifts away; gorges and chasms yawn;
peninsulas stretch to archipelagos;
plateaus, mountains, headlands
crumble and spread to planes, which then
rise to peaks, volcanoes, airy table-lands:
stories in cloud, enframed, entrancing,
so that the bird flashing diagonally down
was merely an interruption of worlds evolving,
of geographies erupting from their own
disintegrations, in minutes, in slow motion.

Sometimes, when the window is blank
as the mind that gazes on it, a point appears
from nowhere and slowly etches a white
parallel across the blue squares.

Silence

Two in a room. Two in a room, and silence,
Except for a steady creaking as she writes
And the slowly turning pages of his book—
She does not ask the title, being gone
Far away with friends he does not know,
Talking across a table, which becomes
The table where she writes about her life
And his, versions he might not recognize;
And when he looks up from the page she's not
Someone who sits there writing, but a girl
He conjures up inside the room, and he
Is not there either, but inside the book
Open on the desk on which he leans.
They are alone, not as two lonely people
Who talk to stop the silence, but as two
Joined by the silence between them, in a room
Whose only sounds define the lack of sound,
The wordless space enveloping them both.

For Carole

Too young for memories like these,
Of girls I never got,
And of the few girls who got me...
Is this how the rot
Sets in, the mind crumbling around
The life unlived, or lived badly?

This is the threshold then, marriage,
Where the stories vanish
Into vistas of blank page
On page of married bliss.
And we are young; prospects for age
Are even hazier than this.

Those memories!—such poor
Attempts in candlelit soirées
To dazzle would-be girl-friends; or
Those times when, feeling bored,
I sagged beneath a rain of chat.
I wonder that we ever met!

And yet we did!—and still we meet
Daily in these areas
Of silences and doubt, no treaty
Signed. My thoughts retreat
Sometimes to past certainty.
I know our love is incomplete—

And will I hope stay so. Completion
Has no renewal. I wish
I could say this more openly,
Bring my words to a flourish.
But love is a truce sometimes,
A continuous meeting each other half-way.

Paediatric Ward

Those who never made it
into the open—whose last
breath was oxygen that had not
slammed doors, rustled leaves,

who gave up the ghost
with hardly a gasp—
cluster to the pane, noses
pressing the glass, hands

waving less and less.
Down corridors the childless
wear masks; you can see them
any day in the street

not window-gazing,
eyes straight on as if
to meet someone they
know will not be there.

Surviving Twin

You run at it. It runs with you.
You try to stamp it out. It stamps too.
You wave. It waves back cheekily.
It belongs to you, and you only,
and though vanishing in bad weather or at night
returns to confront you in broad daylight
at abrupt walls or climbing impossible trees.
It may dart behind you or disappear over ridges,
but turns up again bubbling along hedges,
as irrepressible as you.

These lines were meant to show
that death clings like your shadow,
and, deepening life's colours,
lengthens toward night, as the years pass.

But you ran off with the poem
and with death also.

Travels with my Daughter

All her day's confusions
and frustrations at rest,
she curls up on my stomach.
I stroke her absent-mindedly,
recalling her latest
makeshift remarks:

"The broken moon", its phases
fragments of a smashed toy,
our plane a giant nursery
high over playdough hills:
since for her everything is new
she takes the new for granted;
space is to be flown through
and the small is as big as the large—
her arcs, when she swings "higher
daddy higher" with the hypnotic
push of my hands on her haunches
to make her toes touch the sky,
are more than transatlantic flight.

"The sky is falling",
it's time for bed.
I hunt her slippers
and wedge them on her feet:
not glass, not any prince—
but she's content,
for now at any rate.

Old Year, New Year

A police-car flashed over the carpet,
hit a foot, edged along the hall skirting,
disappeared into the understair dark;
an intercity express tripped into cushions;
a helicopter lunged at the end of a wire.
On television diesel congealed; abandoned lorries
lined up in drifts across Europe;
planes fed sheep and cut-off villages.
An uncle slept in the bay-window, surrounded by snow.
Pine-needles sprinkled the floor;
pullovers bristled and pricked.
For three days after the twelfth
the tree has stood looking in,
bare except for a forgotten chocolate.

The old year shuffles out,
turnip-nose and brussel-sprout buttons
rotting on the lawn, walking-stick erect
above a sooty snow-cone, coal-eyes unreflecting.
We tuck ourselves in and listen to the drip drip.

Garden Anger

My anger will not still.
I bide my time; I feel
My body ripening
Into a brittle shell,

Passion alive within.
The manners friends must make
For friendship's sake are cruel
If they can never break:

Beneath my genial warmth
The anger bursts—a pod
Exploding in the sun,
The seeds cast on the sod.

Repressions

We just missed the doe and buck
that shot across our high-beam, but with brake
slammed hard and wheels slithering, we hit
the fawn that followed. We drove off, dented.

—Or that time we had coffee
in a run-down sea-side café:
while I looked blankly out of the window
and thought what a drab way to earn a living,
cooking for trippers off-season,
you talked to the widowed owner about how
last summer her two-year-old had drowned.
As we left I avoided her eye.

Small deaths... the compliments
we mean to pay but don't,
or that time we flared up for no reason
that I could see—to this day.

Acacia
for M.I.

So large a hole to bury those roots
bunched in sacking and criss-cross sisal,
ready to prise open the soil we pitched
into heaps that seemed too big to put back.

We lowered the sapling; you shovelled
while I held up the spindly trunk
and sighted against horizon and house-front,
nervously circling to check it went straight up;

hammered in a stout bamboo for the first months,
tamped all round with a log end... And here
it stands, lollipop tree that has changed the known
skyline by an inch or two each year:

a memory, imperceptibly grown tall.

Stone-relief, Housesteads

Mediterranean, alien,
stone-flesh chafed
and chastened, whipped
by wind, by hail,
dissolved in rain, till legs
shrank to spindles
and quiver hung
awkwardly from shy
shoulders—or did
the carver's bare hands
shiver, and the chisel
stop too soon?
However it was,
this meagre figure
is our knock-kneed Diana,
our uncomfortable, chill
madonna of the North.

Blind Pianist

His posture is listening—
not to a landscape of images
where notes rush in rapids
and a waterfall, then dwindle
in high trills to a stream,
where octaves are vistas,
and darkening passages
lead to the eerie minor—
but to the sound alone
where dark and light are tones
without colour. He leans
into his mirror of music,
his ruminant medium.

Church-wall

Strands of an organ-voluntary, the lonely
practice of a Saturday, float
from the church, tangling
with traffic and pungent street-smells.

This wall of shining flints has no rules.
Masons, skilled at knapping, once tapped
flints with patient trowels, feeling
for seams, and split them with no effort,
accurately. They reveal
shapes that come as in dreams,
known before, unrecognized till seen.
It is a skill trained and intuitive.

Each irregular stone-face is a rounded
hollow or rounded belly,
and holds in its centre a sun:
in many incarnations one sun shines
along this wall, that, lithe as flesh,
flexes and flashes beside the raucous street—

rough harmony that breaks, and swells again.